ORANGE

By AMANDA DOERING
Illustrations by GLENN THOMAS
Music by DREW TEMPERANTE

CANTATA
LEARNING

WWW.CANTATALEARNING.COM

CANTATA LEARNING

Published by Cantata Learning
1710 Roe Crest Drive
North Mankato, MN 56003
www.cantatalearning.com

Library of Congress Cataloging-in-Publication Data
Names: Doering, Amanda F., 1980– author. | Thomas, Glenn, illustrator. |
    Temperante, Drew, composer.
Title: Orange / by Amanda Doering ; illustrated by Glenn Thomas ; music by
    Drew Temperante.
Description: North Mankato, MN : Cantata Learning, [2018] | Series: Sing your
    colors! | Audience: Ages 4–7. | Audience: K to grade 3. | Includes lyrics
    and sheet music. | Includes bibliographical references.
Identifiers: LCCN 2017017520 (print) | LCCN 2017037926 (ebook) | ISBN
    9781684101658 (ebook) | ISBN 9781684101276 (hardcover : alk. paper) | ISBN
    9781684101986 (pbk. : alk. paper)
Subjects: LCSH: Orange (Color)--Juvenile literature. | Colors--Juvenile
    literature. | Children's songs, English.
Classification: LCC QC495.5 (ebook) | LCC QC495.5 .D6285 2018 (print) | DDC
    535.6--dc23
LC record available at https://lccn.loc.gov/2017017520

Book design and art direction, Tim Palin Creative
Editorial direction, Kellie M. Hultgren
Music direction, Elizabeth Draper
Music arranged and produced by Drew Temperante

Printed in the United States of America in North Mankato, Minnesota.
122017   0378CGS18

ACCESS THE MUSIC!

SCAN CODE WITH MOBILE APP

CANTATALEARNING.COM

TIPS TO SUPPORT LITERACY AT HOME

WHY READING AND SINGING WITH YOUR CHILD IS SO IMPORTANT

Daily reading with your child leads to increased academic achievement. Music and songs, specifically rhyming songs, are a fun and easy way to build early literacy and language development. Music skills correlate significantly with both phonological awareness and reading development. Singing helps build vocabulary and speech development. And reading and appreciating music together is a wonderful way to strengthen your relationship.

READ AND SING EVERY DAY!

TIPS FOR USING CANTATA LEARNING BOOKS AND SONGS DURING YOUR DAILY STORY TIME

1. As you sing and read, point out the different words on the page that rhyme. Suggest other words that rhyme.

2. Memorize simple rhymes such as Itsy Bitsy Spider and sing them together. This encourages comprehension skills and early literacy skills.

3. Use the questions in the back of each book to guide your singing and storytelling.

4. Read the included sheet music with your child while you listen to the song. How do the music notes correlate to the words of the song?

5. Sing along on the go and at home. Access music by scanning the QR code on each Cantata book, or by using the included CD. You can also stream or download the music for free to your computer, smartphone, or mobile device.

Devoting time to daily reading shows that you are available for your child. Together, you are building language, literacy, and listening skills.

Have fun reading and singing!

Orange is a **secondary color**. That means it is made by mixing two **primary colors**. Red and yellow mixed together make orange. Orange is a **warm color** that gives us energy!

Turn the page to go on an orange **adventure**. Don't forget to sing along!

Let's go on an orange adventure!
What orange do you see?

Let's go on an orange adventure!
Show the orange to me!

We need orange to play this game.

We eat a fruit with the same name.

Orange is **prowling** at the zoo.
Orange can be playful, too!

Let's go on an orange adventure!
What orange do you see?

Let's go on an orange adventure!
Show the orange to me!

Orange tells us which roads are closed.
Orange warns us where not to go.

ROAD
CLOSED

15

Orange is most fun in the fall,
with jack-o'-lanterns short and tall.

In winter when the cold wind blows, orange can make a snowman nose.

18

We went on an orange adventure!
What orange did you see?

We went on an orange adventure!
Show your orange to me!

SONG LYRICS
Orange

Let's go on an orange adventure!
What orange do you see?
Let's go on an orange adventure!
Show the orange to me!

We need orange to play this game.
We eat a fruit with the same name.

Orange is prowling at the zoo.
Orange can be playful, too!

Let's go on an orange adventure!
What orange do you see?
Let's go on an orange adventure!
Show the orange to me!

Orange tells us which roads are closed.
Orange warns us where not to go.

Orange is most fun in the fall,
with jack-o'-lanterns short and tall.

In winter when the cold wind blows,
orange can make a snowman nose.

We went on an orange adventure!
What orange did you see?
We went on an orange adventure!
Show your orange to me!

Orange

Pop/Hip Hop
Drew Temperante

Chorus

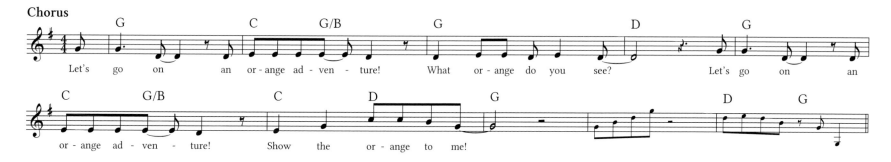

Let's go on an or-ange ad-ven - ture! What or-ange do you see? Let's go on an

or-ange ad-ven - ture! Show the or-ange to me!

Verse

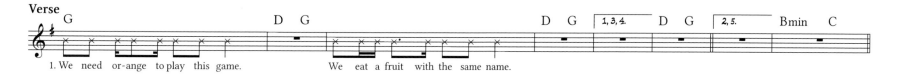

1. We need or-ange to play this game. We eat a fruit with the same name.

Verse 2
Orange is prowling at the zoo.
Orange can be playful, too!

Chorus

Verse 3
Orange tells us which roads are closed.
Orange warns us where not to go.

Verse 4
Orange is most fun in the fall,
with jack-o'-lanterns short and tall.

Verse 5
In winter when the cold wind blows,
orange can make a snowman nose.

Outro

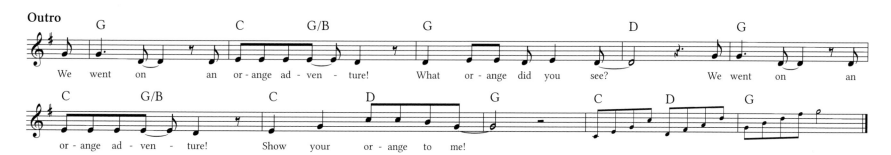

We went on an or-ange ad-ven - ture! What or-ange did you see? We went on an

or-ange ad-ven - ture! Show your or-ange to me!

GLOSSARY

adventure—an exciting experience

primary colors—colors, such as blue, red, and yellow, mixed to make other colors

prowling—moving in a sneaky way, like a wild animal

secondary colors—colors, such as orange, green, and purple, made by mixing two primary colors

warm color—bold and exciting colors that we see in nature, such as reds, yellows, and oranges

GUIDED READING ACTIVITIES

1. Looking back at the pictures in this story, what orange things do you see? Can you find these orange things: an oriole (a type of bird), a monarch butterfly, carrots, and traffic cones?

2. People sometimes connect colors to their emotions. What feeling or feelings does orange make you think of? Why?

3. Go on an orange adventure through your home. Then grab your markers or crayons and draw pictures of the orange things you found.

TO LEARN MORE

Borth, Teddy. *Orange Animals*. Minneapolis: Abdo Kids, 2015.

Ghigna, Charles. *The Wonders of the Color Wheel*. North Mankato, MN: Capstone, 2014.

Rustad, Martha E. H. *Orange Foods*. North Mankato, MN: Capstone, 2017.

Shores, Erika L. *Pumpkins*. North Mankato, MN: Capstone, 2016.